Another Beautiful Day Indoors

Another Beautiful Day Indoors

Erik Kennedy

TE HERENGA WAKA
UNIVERSITY PRESS

Te Herenga Waka University Press
Victoria University of Wellington
PO Box 600 Wellington
teherengawakapress.co.nz

Te Herenga Waka University Press
was formerly Victoria University Press.

Copyright acknowledgements on page 93 are an extension
of this imprint page.

A catalogue record is available at the National Library
of New Zealand.

ISBN 9781776920075

Printed by Blue Star, Petone

To George and Susan Kennedy

. . . Vain things alone
Have driven our perverse and aimless band.

—Ernest Dowson, 'A Last Word'

It is utterly decadent, in a world gone out of joint, to behave
as though everything were in perfect order.

—Ernst Fischer, *The Necessity of Art: A Marxist Approach*

A system based on perpetual growth cannot function
without peripheries and externalities. There must always be
an extraction zone—from which materials are taken without
full payment—and a disposal zone, where costs are dumped
in the form of waste and pollution. As the scale of economic
activity increases until capitalism affects everything, from
the atmosphere to the deep ocean floor, the entire planet
becomes a sacrifice zone: we all inhabit the periphery of the
profit-making machine.

—George Monbiot, 'Dare to Declare Capitalism Dead—
Before It Takes Us All Down with It'

Contents

1

Out on the Pleasure Pier

Out on the pleasure pier on that benign afternoon,
the air heavy with the blossom of vinegar and old tyres,
you asked what was the closest I had come to death.

I thought of when I had applied the bolt-cutters
to that big machine's cord.

I considered some inglorious public collapses.

But I didn't know, I said. It was probably
something I wasn't even aware of, I said.
Something that passed me by, like a parcel bound
for Ash Hill instead of Ash Mill, I said.

On the pier, two good-looking people passed us by,
complementing our goodness.
Two ugly people passed us by,
complementing our ugliness.

It could be happening now, you said.

Another scurfy wave glided shoreward languidly.

That's the thing about what you don't know, I said.
It could always be happening now.

Studying the Myth of the Flood

Did it happen all at once,
the buildings filling up
with seawater like rain gauges,
litter and people floating
into the mountain ranges
between lunch and teatime?

Or did it happen in deep time,
an imperceptible going-under,
a welcoming of the dark
onto the land, no need for an ark
for a resigned people
distracted by other hatreds?

This is what the future,
if there is one, will wonder.

Microplastics in Antarctica

Samples of snow collected during the same expedition were analysed by an independent laboratory for the presence of perfluorinated chemicals, widely used as water-proofing and grease-proofing chemicals in outdoor clothing and food packaging. Some can be carried over vast distances on air currents and deposited in rain or snowfall, far from their sources.
—University of Exeter press release, 8 June 2018

The snow contains a finer snow.
That's how it gets there, this plastic
that maybe once kept a lettuce green
or packaged another plastic package.

Scratch the scalp of civilisation
and bits of it go all over the place.
Concerned about those embarrassing flakes?
You should be.

We are everywhere. We're even where
we don't want to be.
It's like being a celebrity
for being stupid: your likeness on buses,

you hardly knowing why.
I could cry with respect
for our reckless tenacity
the way I laugh at sad films.

Eleven babies have been born in Antarctica,
all of them healthy human babies
and not trash golems come to avenge
the spited Earth.

Yet. The oldest baby is forty now.
He has seen what we do,
and how.
Can we be worse than we already are?

Somewhere in the miles-deep ice
an answer is frozen,
and I hope, hope, hope we quit
before we get to it.

Satellite Insurance

Believe it or not
there are people
who get up and go to work
every day
in the satellite insurance sector

because a lot of things
can go wrong with
or happen to
a satellite
misfortunes that cost millions of dollars
and involve
pieces of space junk
scorching through the atmosphere
and the clouds
and ultimately people's roofs and floors

and then
if you're the satellite owner
you've got a situation on your hands
because you've frightened a nice couple senseless
and very rudely incinerated
their carpets and cellar
and the satellite certainly won't
be the same again either

but it's okay
because you've got a policy
in a drawer somewhere
and there's a voice at the other end of a hotline
a voice that's practised and reassuring
because it knew this day would come

because if micrometeoroids
or lasers or hackers
don't take down a satellite
well there's always that wily old trapper orbital decay
who has been laying unnoticed snares

and the voice on the satellite insurance hotline asks
accident or attack
and you say you don't know
you don't know how
your beautiful satellite
came to grief

and the voice says
that's all right
it's not always easy to tell
sometimes 'the enemy' is an enemy
and sometimes 'the enemy' is the universe itself

but we'll get to the bottom of it

we always do

The Please Stop Killing Us and Destroying Everything That Sustains Us Society

Hello, everyone, and welcome to the first meeting of the Please Stop Killing Us and Destroying Everything That Sustains Us Society.

I know that some people feel that organisation and protest are not the correct responses to recent events, including the events that involve us being killed and everything that sustains us being destroyed. Some people would have you believe that we need to go through the official channels if we expect our demands to end the slaughter and spoliation to be taken seriously. Some people maintain that, in a way, *we* are the ones who are killing and destroying when we call out those who kill us and destroy everything that sustains us.

Respectfully, I disagree.

As I look around this room, I see the amiable faces of friends, as inviting as warm bread. I see into your comradely hearts, as fruitful as a well full of mulled wine. And I know that it would be a betrayal of this fellowship of the yet-unexpunged if we did not say politely and without embarrassment: please stop killing us and destroying everything that sustains us.

It may seem incredible that there are still some who have not heard our message, some who do not realise that we are dying and that we would like to stop dying. But it is the case. This is our work.

I am proud to stand before you tonight and say that maybe, if anyone listens to us, we will be the last ones to die. Maybe we will be the ones to stop this world turning to custard, to toxic caramel or poisonous butterscotch. And maybe, should our cause not be favoured, we can write the guilt of our persecutors into history, and the good etiquette of our struggle can inspire the next generation of irked petitioners.

Thank you. You're welcome to stay for a chat and some of the refreshments we have left.

The Safety Coffin

You know those bells
that eccentric people
used to have rigged
into their coffins
so if they weren't really dead
and they woke up panicked
in the dark
in their best clothes
they could grab the bell-pull
and some freelance grave monitor
at the surface
would hear the tinkling
and hopefully
dig them up?

That, but for love.

So if an apparently dead feeling
comes to
with a jolt
sometime after it has been seen to expire,
after it has been prepared and dressed,
put in a box,
kissed goodbye,
and lowered into the earth,
let it have a final chance
to live
before it's forgotten by everybody,
before it suffocates,
having scratched its fingers bloody
on the inside of the lid.

To a Couple Who Had Their Rings Brought to the Altar by Drone at Their Garden Wedding

I'll say this for you: you're unafraid of mockery
and the coldly irritable judgements of posterity.
You're unafraid of accusations of faddishness.
You're possibly unafraid of technology itself.
And, most impressively, you're unafraid of the wind,
which bucked the drone almost to ringlessness.
It was a katabatic wind that brought a chill
to the wedding party and unnerved the nerveless
among the guests. It was just an everyday wind, really,
a Saturday gust that wouldn't have troubled
a pair of ring-bearing kids dressed like elderly dove-breeders
in their flat caps and braces, or like Arts and Crafts fairies
with acanthus-embroidered cushions and Celtic buttons.
But the drone felt the drama in the wind,
and the drone alone knew how to fit it into
this day that you say is a whole life in miniature.
It's time for the presents. The quadcopter operator
offers the pitch and yaw. The caterers offer the rolls.
The only perfect rhyme for 'lover' is 'lover'.
Go forth and hover.

The Black Friday Elegy

I have a vision of a thin man
who only wanted some socks
being torn limb from limb
in a shopping centre

what an adventure

he never stood a chance

he wandered into a war dance
and was separated into his component parts
like a beam of light
split by a prism

but at least he died doing what he loved
complaining about capitalism

Another Beautiful Day Indoors

The light lengthens on the carpet,
a sure symptom of afternoon.
I haven't left the house today
because there's only one reason
to do that, and I've already got goat cheese.
A half moon is only a quarter of the moon.
This sky should win trophies.
I look at other people, their energy,
and think they must have been raised by marmots.
I know for the sake of social cohesion
we must try to live togetherly,
like Bronze Age women and men,
but it's been a long week, and, anyway,
petrol prices have gone up again.

The First Plant Grown on the Moon

In memory of the cotton plant grown on the lunar lander
Chang'e 4, *January 2019*

The first plant grown on the moon was already dead
by the time we heard it had been alive.
That's no way to treat a crew member.
Space agencies make rubbish mourners.

The cotton plant was just following orders.
The order was: *Die in the lunar night.*
Die when it gets below minus one hundred.
Confine Officer Cotton Plant's corpse to quarters.

There's no explorer like a dead explorer.
There's no place like a 'moon surface micro-ecological circle'.
The radiance of life is an impossible product.
We are its exporters.

The moon is full of foreigners,
with our stiff flags and our left-behind shit.
Some corner of a foreign field will be forever
Earth. Let us tend to it.

Open-Plan Office

What you may not know is that
this office was modelled on heaven.
Fluorescent, expansive, unchanging.
Other options were considered
that offered privacy or walls
or a courtyard for smokers, but no,
we thought heaven represented us best.
It's a Protestant heaven, obviously,
in which anyone can talk to anyone else
across the open space and white desks,
the big spaces and the whitest desks
which represent all of time
and also all the time we have
for each other in this office.
Ask Quentin for a thumbtack
and see what he says. He's never too busy.
Talk to Sophie about the game
even though she sits behind you
and hates all the games—
she gives so much of herself.
Don't you feel terrible now
having imposed on Sophie,
dear Sophie who once braided your hair
after that horrible meeting?
Please don't. Sophie and Quentin
and you and I are behaving
just as we should. Rightness
is in the air, coming through
the white vents at 21°C,
and that sharp smell you smell,
like a printer with a bullet through it,

is the aether, which surrounds us
and supports us and helps us to glow.

The Class Anxiety Country Song

I pull into the station,
tell them where I'm headed,
ask which has fewer calories,
diesel or unleaded.

I'm leaving behind a heartbreak,
a boy by the name of Regan.
I thought he was a Libra
and he thought honey was vegan.

I'm fixing to go up north,
where the stars are cold and quavery,
to a town with no pretensions
and a juice bar and a bakery,

and maybe I'll find love there.
I know that I'll be looking—
for a boy with cinnamon hair
who reads Murray Bookchin.

And if I don't come back
it's because I'm somewhere better,
with a boy and some land and a cat
and drugs and an Irish setter.

I 3D-printed a banjo
to play this scratchy song.
If the easy way is right,
then God, he made me wrong.

Picking up Pieces of Paper
Other People Have Dropped

If I was capable of learning lessons
or believed in human nature
I could learn some lessons
about human nature

from the bits of themselves
people have lost
on the pavement
or in a hallway

a funeral programme
for someone named Gaia
who died on her birthday
(which was Earth Day)

a receipt for a sex toy
stating 'NO RETURNS'
next to which someone has written
'fuck this'

or a one-item shopping list reading
'TO GET: nothing'
not nothing written there
but the word 'nothing'

Phosphate from Western Sahara

*[New Zealand fertiliser companies are the only significant remaining foreign
buyers of phosphate from Moroccan-controlled Western Sahara.]*

It travels along the world's longest conveyor belt
surrounded by the world's longest minefield.
Each mine says, '*My* field, *my* field, *my* field.'
It travels to the land that fertiliser built.
Sorry, Western Sahara, New Zealand needs this.
Phosphate is purveyed like a louche commodity, like a white kiss,
like a lost memory of self-determination.
Two peoples trapped in a laughable half-rhyme: Sahrawis, Kiwis.
It remains our position that we are operating within UN expectations—
this is the accounting software justification
of abstracted minds, which apologise and at the same time race
to take what a dying industry makes. Thanks, free marketeers.
'Peak phosphorus' in thirty years,
and until then this comedy carnival ride of equivocations and rocks.
You can see the phosphate dust from space,
like a tantrum in a sandbox.
You don't have to look hard for motives
when someone guards their shame with barrenness and explosives.

Focus Group Survivor

Was I mostly bored or mostly poor?

Or maybe I was just lonely.

Hell is ten people trying to name a car.

Something soothing or stirring or botanical or Latin.

Boronia. Pronghorn. Eleganza. Marconi.

Faunus. Quiver. Amethyst. Satin.

I, on the other hand, wanted something solid and wooden,

something that says 'I will survive a crash'.

Like acorns, I swept up names in clusters.

Dugong. Barrel. Halberd. Pudding.

Whipsmart. Stoutheart. Norfolk. Mustard.

There is more to focus than concentration.

At least they paid in cash.

At least I know my limitations.

Van Advertising 'Interior Plantscaping Services'

Tear up the floorboards of the sexiest room,
dig down into the life-giving loam,
and plant a bed of red hot pokers
to entice the bees, the bees, the bees.
That's what I'm hearing. Let the knife racks
of the kitchen be full of succulents of many shapes
and degrees of spikiness. Pack the living room
with living testaments to your elegance,
with philodendrons and umbrella trees
and whatever looks good with Antoine Griezmann
scoring on successive Saturdays on your TV,
because style and sport belong together now
under the canopy of your verdant roomscape.
That's what they're saying—they're all saying it
in this industry of plantscapes and brandscapes,
inside houses and offices and human brainscapes.
They say it because it's true and it's good
and it's vital to the contemporary joyscape.
So escape with us into the easy luxury and peace
of your own home. May it never end.
May contentment fill your ever-cleaner air.
May it never end. There's a discount
if you recommend us to a friend.

An Interesting Redundancy Package

Success is the second-best revenge
after revenge,
which is the best revenge.
I have turned the other cheek
until I was an ornate cylinder
of turned cheeks,
peach-coloured and weird,
like a sixties lampshade.

And I have succeeded
on my own terms, oh yes.
What else do you call it
when I rescue every single earthworm
I see on the pavement
after a brisk rain?
And surely it is success
to have made many people strangely happy
with words,
like a theologian who has translated
the entire Bible
into Christmas cracker jokes.
I have dignity-enhancing achievements like these
in many fields.

But the terms of my success are not terms
my adversary understands.
I'm performing in the wrong arena.
I am a beluga singing
to a vacuum cleaner.

Which is why you find me here,
at the corner

of Revenge Street and Revenge Parkway,
planting contraband
in my former manager's office,
an action which—
to judge by the fact that I'm full of
adrenaline to my twitching earlobes—
is also success.

Lives of the Poets

There is the possible world in which,
having no safety net
to fall into, I killed myself.

There is the world in which
acclaim came early
with a book called something like
Sex Owls of the Sun,
and the effects of success jaded me,
so I stopped pursuing
the art that I loved.

And there is also the world that was
a succession of cool, forgettable evenings
spent among canapés and loud friends,
in which we aged so slowly
that we hardly noticed it,
until it blurred our vision
like damp creeping into a camera.

The Inertia Poem

You've been in love for so long
that you count your partner's prepositions
for fun, and you know that his favourite Blind Lemon
    Jefferson song
is 'Peach Orchard Mama',
and you'd rather be dropped from a long-range bomber
over Pyongyang than risk what you've got.
But maybe you want to be more than compatible.
One thing to do
would be to stock your bedroom with hoods and clamps and
    whips and ropes.
Another would be to tie your wishes and hopes
into a sexy balloon animal.
Decisions, decisions.
Or maybe, just for once, go to a nice restaurant.
Only two out of seventeen options are vegetarian.
You feel sick looking at the menu's font.
Like one of those nineteenth-century antiquarians
who was also a vicar,
you don't know how to want the new.
Some things are just not what they're not.
Splitting up would be quicker.

All Holidays Are Made-Up Holidays

I don't think we were ever happier
than on Cabinet Day, when we went along
from house to house hanging little doors
around each other's necks to hide our secrets.
It was the perfect winter holiday of childhood,
when malfeasance and desire both
were masked by smells of baking cakes, of fennel,
aniseed, and cloves.
                              On the other hand,
we only understood the Feast of the Holy Indifference
when we were older. Some years it was in May,
some in June. The fête would last as long
as one candle burned. The Indifference Queen
or King, if there was one, soothed us with a dance
danced sitting down, in silence. This was how
we learned a single-minded lassitude.
                                        Which brings us to
the pagan rites of Multifunctionalia.
This holiday, they say, replaced still other
older, darker festivals, all hoofs and genitals
and welts and berries! In our time it was still
an orgy of party-hopping, wrapping beds
in coloured plastic, hanging out of cars
shouting jokes we'd written. There was so much
to do. It filled the summer like a dirty job,
just like it was supposed to.

2

[notes towards a definition of essential work]

... Like heartbreak.
Work structures so much life.

—Wendy Trevino, Sonnet 24 in 'Popular Culture
& Cruel Work'

Capitalism does not produce its own gravediggers.

—G.A. Cohen, *If You're an Egalitarian, How Come
You're So Rich?*

Four Life Forms

I was having an affair with my partner's therapist, and she was having an affair with mine. It didn't feel great. For a start, I suspected that her therapist must have heard some pretty damaging misrepresentations of me. The Copenhagen holiday. The Volkswagen Dealership Incident. I sometimes thought that I could see the fires of judgement flickering in the backs of her therapist's eyes when we met for chess and sex in her dim garden flat. Even worse, I had poured poison about my partner into the ear of *my* therapist for six years, and he still managed to fancy her. What sort of person could like the woman I had described? A woman who had done the casual evils I had accused her of? According to me, she was a clonal colony of malice covering dozens of acres. My therapist either didn't believe me or thought that she was worth the risk. I understood this. Because I had felt that way once, and who's to say, if we're being honest, that I wasn't mostly to blame for what happened? That I wasn't the epidemic that triggers the extinction event? Not long after I discontinued therapy, I heard from a friend that our therapists, Graham and Tayla, had started a relationship of their own and were moving to Sydney together. I understood this, too. All in all, I had a lot to occupy my thoughts in the long nights after I moved my things out of the house and started secretly sleeping in my lab.

Setting up the Debate

I was putting out the chairs for the debate that night. A woman from one of the campaigns came up to me and asked, 'Is there an odd number of chairs?' I said, 'I don't know. Does it matter?' 'Yes. Neither of the candidates will take the stage tonight if there isn't an odd number of chairs for the audience.' 'But that's crazy,' I said. 'Well my candidate is crazy. Not sure about the other one, but mine is like a floor covered in mousetraps. He's serious about the chair thing. He also holds singing meetings on Fridays.' 'Singing meetings?' 'Anyone who has anything to say has to sing it.' 'That sounds beautiful,' I said. 'It is. We want to bring beauty back into politics. So make sure you put out an odd number of chairs. And put one of these on each seat.' She handed me a stack of A5 flyers. All they said, in 72-point Impact, was 'VOTE, YOU MORONS'. 'Is this beautiful?' I asked. 'Beauty doesn't have to be nice,' she said.

Official Printer to the Government

I was in the public square putting up a poster of a soon-to-be-executed traitor. It was hard to find space on the Wall of Proclamations, so I had to cover the poster of a recently executed traitor. Lucky him, his infamy papered over so quickly. A lark-like woman crossed the square towards me. 'Are you Ms Houllier who used to teach at School No. 76?' she asked. I admitted it. 'You taught my son fifteen years ago,' she said, and named him. The sort of kid who wore a scarf like a nappy. I asked how the lad was doing. Executed as a traitor, apparently. 'It's not because of anything I taught him,' I said defensively. 'I didn't say that it was,' she replied. We gave each other the three-fingered wave of the regime and went about our business. I thought about how being an official printer to the government was like being a teacher to the citizenry. I thought about how publishing the deeds of the condemned was like correcting papers. It was an appallingly hot day—too hot, really, for the crowd that would turn up at the two o'clock executions. Good thing, then, that my partner Anna would be in the square soon to open her kiosk selling floppy hats and sun cream.

Agatha and Florian

I'd spent the summer in my wingsuit setting records: farthest horizontal wingsuit flight, first person to fly under the Glenfinnan Viaduct in a wingsuit, things like that.

To celebrate my achievements, my sponsor, Inventox, held a little do in my honour in Zürich. Inventox was a pharmaceutical company pushing a new prescription-strength party drink sold in grenade-size yellow cans. Conviviality blossomed like an evening primrose.

I was pleased when a familiar-looking woman, dressed all in yellow and wearing a yellow wig, introduced herself by saying, 'I'm a big fan of your work.'

'My work is partying until 6am!' I said in English, translating my Swiss sponsor's popular slogan. 'That and setting wingsuit records.' Her name was Agatha, pronounced the South American way.

'I mean your work as a cabinet-maker,' Agatha said. 'Or have you forgotten, Florian?'

Now, only six people alive knew that I, the wingsuit daredevil Stefan König, was also Florian Moser, formerly a maker of cabinets for magicians, and none of them were in Zürich.

A server walked by with a tray of fizzing yellow cocktails. I took two glasses: Agatha's first drink, my eighth.

I stayed silent, like a tree forcing itself not to sway. 'Don't worry,' Agatha said. 'I won't tell anyone. But you're needed. There has been a disappearance in a magician's cabinet. It was at a children's birthday party at the mountain hideaway of a notorious autocrat. I'm sure I don't need to name him.'

I focused with an effort as she continued. My sponsor's colours jaundiced the room.

'One of the missing children is the autocrat's only daughter, the Most Benevolent and Respected Flower of the Revolution. It has been snowing for a week, and there is no road access.'

'Will I need my wingsuit?' I asked, just as Inventox's beaming CFO beckoned me to the stage to say a few words.

The Planned Obsolescence Rhapsody

The mayor of the town came up to me in my smithy carrying a hessian sack full of clanking metal. He disgorged its contents on a table.

'Reinhold,' he said, 'I'm sorry to have to say this, but I've been fielding complaints from some of the townsfolk about your workmanship.'

'My workmanship is at the highest standard, Mr Mayor,' I said. 'I forge the hardest nails and the thickest chains in the district. I'm well known for it.'

'Well, precisely.' He fingered a door hinge. 'The fact is there's another blacksmith in the next village who is making shonky items, and people love it. His productions fail unexpectedly. Hoe blades are breaking off in the ground. Horses have to be reshod every week. The hoops on casks are bursting and flooding people's floors with wine. It's new. It's exciting. If people are going to spend their hard-earned money on bits of iron, they want something more than unshowy durability. That's the message I'm getting. The town is gaining a reputation as a place that's unfriendly to progress.'

'What do you want me to do about it?'

'I don't know, Reinhold. I don't know. Think about it, and I'll come see you again next week.' The mayor took his empty sack and walked off down the road.

The way I saw it, I had three options. I could take on an incompetent apprentice. I could work drunk. Or I could burn down the smithy, collect on the insurance, and start again in a new trade.

I battered out a pair of tongs then stood with my face to the heat of the forge, squinting, trying to discern omens in the shimmering air. Maybe there was a fourth option. I saw the form of a scheme materialising in a column of the updraught. I arched the spot where my eyebrows would have been had they not been singed off.

Yes, that just might succeed. And this is how I came up with the idea of selling a tool that could be used to destroy my handiwork. Something savage for warping a decorative railing or crushing a trowel. The other blacksmith was relying on chance to break his creations; I was empowering my customers to break mine themselves. The great age of the individual was coming, and I was doing my part to shape its course.

The Plot of the Nativity Play

A bright new star appeared in the sky. My friends Balthazar, Caspar, and Melchior thought it was shining over Bethlehem.

'I'm not so sure about that,' I said. 'I think it could be over Athens, or maybe Augsburg.'

'Of course it's over Bethlehem. You think I don't know where Bethlehem is?' asked Balthazar. I said nothing.

'The star could betoken the coming of an infant god. Perhaps we're being touched by the breath of something holy,' said Caspar.

'We could bring gifts. Gold, frankincense, and myrrh,' said Melchior.

'No one likes myrrh,' I said. Now it was my friends' turn to be silent.

We crossed the trackless wastes, buffeted by foul winds, menaced by mysterious temptations. We passed skeletons: dog, camel, human.

It was an awful trip, dirty, tedious, and uncomfortable, and I wasn't shy about saying so. B., C., and M. mollified me with ecstatic flimflam. We were journeying deep into the country of belief, they said. Destiny was guiding our feet into the way of peace.

After a number of days, we arrived at the gates of Bethlehem and spoke to a watchman. Had anything noteworthy happened in the city recently?

'A child has been born to Mary and Joseph, a young couple who have just moved here from Nazareth,' the watchman said.

Anything else?

'The pub up the road is doing a two-for-one fish and chips night tonight,' he said.

'Okay, my friends,' I said, 'you were right. This is a miracle.'

The star we had followed was blazing directly overhead, shrinking our shadows almost to nothing.

Early Evening at the Coal Plant

I was all alone at the coal plant. The final hour of the day had gone by quietly, like a horse wearing slippers. As my co-workers processed out, I said: *bye, Rolf—bye, Elaine—bye, Barry—bye, Ed—bye, Lakshmi.* No one made me leave even though I was never the last one out. Where was the night shift?

I didn't know if I should stay or go or what to do, so I watered some sick plants. I rolled a screw in slightly unpredictable circles on a table. This made me thoughtful. I thought about how I had got work at the coal plant by accident. My one real qualification was that I was very good at shovelling. If I had made different choices I would probably be shovelling manure or shovelling snow or shovelling soil into graves. I imagined that scientists who wind up making biological weapons must feel the way I do, that their powers have been misappropriated by shadowy forces. Scientists and me, both destroying the world against our wills, like rice water foaming out of the pot.

Notes Towards a Definition
of Essential Work

Since we stopped going outside, I hadn't had a proper haircut for months. Luckily, I knew a guy who knew a guy who knew a guy on the dark web who could do clandestine styling. My details were sent on to Ivan, who messaged me to say that he had six haircuts' worth of experience and an immunity certificate proving that he had already had the virus.

We met at 5am on the dry bit of waste ground between the bog and the windmill. Ivan's handsome, kind face made him the sort of person you'd trust to look after your coffee while you duck into the loo. He was wearing a blue suit and muddy trainers. His tie had an eagle on it and some words in Russian. Judging by the tracks, he had dragged an office chair through the bog. I sat down.

I thought about our collective panic about haircutlessness. It's not as if it's actually dangerous to let your hair grow, but I knew people who were treating each day unshorn as if it were an injury to their immortal souls.

'It's okay if you don't want to talk,' Ivan said. 'Some people don't like to, when they get their hair cut.' I assured him that I did like to talk and asked him how he got into the haircutting game. He said that, since everyone was home all the time, work had kind of dried up in his old line of business.

'What business was that?' I asked.

'Burglary,' he said.

'Was it interesting work?'

'Very.'

'Meet many interesting people?'

'That's the exact thing I usually tried to avoid.'

'Of course,' I said, with what I hoped was an understanding chortle.

Ivan looked off into the eastern sky where the day was announcing itself half-heartedly. 'You know, you spend a lifetime building up a business—developing a vision—and then it all just disappears,' he lamented. 'It's not fair.'

'It certainly sounds unfair,' I said.

To be honest, this conversation was about as good as my average conversation in a barber's chair, and not much stranger. Ivan was scissoring my hair with unexpected grace, like a kayaker in a kiddie pool. I became lost in the thick undergrowth of my thoughts. We must have continued talking, but I was busy imagining Ivan entering the empty homes of the holidaying rich by night with a stocking over his head. Do burglars actually wear stockings over their heads? Probably not. And did Ivan wear a suit while burgling? That seemed impossible, but it would invest the work with a certain appropriate dignity. From a class war perspective, I had respect for the person I hoped Ivan was in his old career. Maybe his burglaries were sophisticated, theoretically grounded surgical strikes against our oppressors. Maybe we needed more people taking a campaign of wealth redistribution out into the community instead of wasting their lives cocooned in jobs in some unnecessary and unhallowed tier of university administration, to give a completely hypothetical example. Imagining Ivan's stealthy trespasses also reminded me of my own vulnerability. Last year we'd given a key to one of the neighbour kids who was cat-sitting for us, but the key had gone missing. I cursed myself for not having changed the locks. An obvious security liability.

'All done,' Ivan said, and showed me the back of my head using a hand mirror and a chrome car bumper that was leaning against a nearby tree. I gave him the universal sign for yeah-I-guess-that'll-do: a nod. He'd done a very good job, actually. I may not have truly needed *a* haircut, but, in hindsight, I needed *this* haircut.

He stooped down to pick up the locks of grey hair that had settled in the ryegrass. 'Do you mind if I keep these?' he asked. 'I've got a business idea. Nothing's going to be the same after this.'

'Nothing's going to be the same,' I agreed.

Ivan heaved the office chair upside down over his shoulders and balanced the seat cushion on the top of his head. He set off across the bog. Ah, so I was wrong about him dragging the chair.

The Night Before the Barn-Raising

It was the night before the barn-raising and our son told us that he wasn't going to be participating. He no longer believed, he told us. I asked him if he meant that he didn't believe in *barns*, and I pointed impatiently to the wall and a print of a lovely old barn in DeKalb County. It wasn't like that, he said. He no longer believed in community, in cooperation. And I said oh, wasn't that convenient for him to give up on community just when the Flowerdews needed his help with their barn. And I asked if he didn't remember when Mrs Flowerdew bought a subscription to *Pigeon Fancy Magazine* when he was fundraising for his school choir trip to Paraguay. And I asked if he thought that Mrs Flowerdew gave an everloving faff about pigeons. The woman is allergic to birds. *Allergic*. She did it to help him, and I said that I shouldn't wonder that she'd do it again even if he'd become a thankless heartbreak to his dear mother and a disappointment to the town and a threat to a cohesive society. He said he was sorry but that's just how it was, and we needed to respect his beliefs, and he was going outside to get some air and he hoped we'd understand some day. So I told his little sister to wait ten minutes then go upstairs and cut all his shoelaces with the kitchen scissors.

The Admin Job Psalm

It was my first day copying manuscripts in the scriptorium. Shafts of light bored through the clerestory windows onto our lecterns. The monk next to me was Oswald, the hairy son of a wool merchant. I saw that Oswald was copying passages on practical holiness, but as he wrote out the Latin faithfully he read out a story about a wolf caught in a snare. He paused to sharpen his quill. When he resumed copying, his theme had changed; he was now declaiming the saga of an army of pyramids at war with an army of spheres.

'Where are these stories coming from, Brother Oswald?' I asked. 'You are the only one who has ever wondered,' he answered. 'This is a safe life, but a long one. I like to pass the time by translating my copy-text into some of the languages I have learned: spite, fear, envy.' He copied out a parable of thrift and recited a narrative about a woman and her lover drowning her husband in the bath.

The dust motes danced in the sunbeams like amoebas. And so we worked.

A month later, Oswald was found hanging in the orchard, motionless among the quinces. In his cell was a note addressed to me: 'To Rufus, who will know how to translate this story into the language of tenderness.'

3

The Foiled Axe Murder Poem

I have only been threatened once with an axe.
It really clarifies your thinking.
Later. It clarifies your thinking *later.*
At the time, your thinking is mostly about being
split open. Opening up.

When you open up to yourself later,
in your axe-less leisure,
you think in the genre of flashbacks,
a counterfactual throwback attack flick,
the shock of what might have been.

The ridiculousness of the scene
was . . . ridiculous. A high, unstable man
promising to sort me out,
me hurrying out into the bitter, brambly night,
haring along, hopping a fence to safety.

I was panting like a treadmill with heart disease.
The only thing more ridiculous
would have been my corpse's essences
oozing into the soil.
Un-accidental axe ooze.

It can only happen once, your axe murder,
and it's impossible to be prepared,
to put your affairs in order,
which puts it in the same category
as other things so horrible

you're certain they could never happen twice,
like blackmail or heartbreak

or malaria or your house burning down
or missing a Christmas Eve flight
or thinking the world's all wrong, and being right.

Young Adult Success Stories

This fantastic article outlines how, at the tender age of twenty-two, Brad got seed money for his underwear delivery start-up and bought a Bugatti. What an amazing tale of industry and sticktoitiveness. How did he do it? Ah, yes, it's right there in paragraph 8—he has rich parents.

I'd also urge you to read about Kaitlyn, who took a gap year to do an internship in the tourism sector in Thailand and managed to save $8,000 of the $200,000 needed for a down payment on an Art Deco bungalow at the seaside. She recently bought the property. What was her secret? Allow me to blow your mind: she has rich parents.

And all you incipient entrepreneurs out there will certainly want to note the example of Sarah Jane, who took her passion for crafting and made it a career. Her knitted hamper covers are a must-have. Now she lives on a horse farm in Devon. Rich parents? That's right, rich parents.

◇ ◇ ◇

O rich parents! you grey eminences of the markets,
you unseen, almost-edited-out powers of feel-good stories,
you assisters in hitting impossible targets,
you producers of inglorious earners and unearned glories,
please parent us as well—the small strugglers of life,
the alienated labour, the up-to-their-eyeballs-in-student-debt
    debtors,
the scrappers who feel like they're sawing timber with a butter
    knife
every day or who download, every morning, a new set of fetters!

O rich parents, parent us, too, in your abstracted and aloof way!
Support us like the lighter-than-air gas that you are,
float us like a pity zeppelin, like a kite above a motorway!
Make the far near and make the ridiculously far less far.
O rich parents, treat us like one of your precious Ruperts
     or Priscillas!
I pray to the even richer superbeings above you,
if you help us, we'll stop calling you parasites and spirit-killers.
We'll do something I think you'll get: society will pretend to
     love you.

There Is a Man Dancing
on the Rudder of an
Enormous Cargo Ship

having arrived as part of a protest flotilla
of kayaks and inflatables and paddleboards,
a semi-cohesive squadron of possibility and guerrilla
tactics that are half surprise party, half interview with the
    parole board,
and his dancing is pretty good, not only for who he is
(barefoot, bearded, handy with a hammer, white)
but for what it means (it's sand thrown in the gears
of an unethical industry—I mean, they're being pretty polite
for water-borne protestors, but they're angry),
and, yeah, the police are hailing him from the quay,
but this doesn't seem to be leading him towards any sudden
    doubts,
he just doesn't seem to care,
and isn't that what dancing is—seeming not to care
about the things you care about?

Local Politics

I just want to know

at the start of every day

forever

if I will see the civic willows

by the river

in the morning mist

and by them

the day's official geese

and swans

busy at their tasks

so I can calibrate myself

and is that so much to ask

The Vegan Poem, or It's Not a Conversion Narrative Because I Was Already Converted

Whatever you do, don't watch
the shocking undercover video
of how we treat the things we eat.
It's all shit and squeals and pus and teats.
The only thing spared is the status quo.
When I watched the video
(so you don't have to)
I turned grey and shadow-beaten
like a hill beset by gusty westerlies.
I shrivelled like fridge celery,
leaking a long slick of sympathy.
I willed myself through my anger,
a crab plodding through treacle
towards the crab-fighting ring.
If I never do anything else,
let me do no harm, I say,
in my best breathless ethicist voice,
and I mean it, come hell
or high water or a wasting disease.
Today, once again, caring seems
to be the less debilitating option,
but it's hard to believe there's hope
for any animal-affirming utopia
when people hate even each other
with the violence of a sneeze.

Nineteenth-Century
Rural Road-Builders

They built roads we still use
to move people we now judge
and things we've replaced
with other, similar things.

They pulled muscles we've forgotten
and worked hours we've outlawed
for bosses we can recognise.
They told the same necessary lies.

They had more interesting curses than 'fuck'.
They loved the views that they made for the future,
for the people who were lucky enough
to be born after them.

We imagine them not complaining,
but they complained.
We imagine them working in the sun
and working harder when it was raining,

sparing our feelings
with their sepia stoicism,
preserving their bad smiles on glass plates
in the drawers of collections.

They built themselves
and they built us
and they built a time
and an idea of time.

They stuck charges in rock faces,
braced, and put their fingers in their ears,
where our fingers are, too,
after all these years.

The Autonomous Vehicle Research Centre

There is only one
really serious philosophical problem
and that is:

do self-driving cars brake for animals?

And the answer is mostly no,
not unless it might damage the vehicle,
depreciating the asset
and taking up time,

and it occurs to us that
the really serious philosophical counterargument
is regiments of

exploding squirrels,
hedgehogs fashioned of filed tungsten,
foxes that release flaming napalm
when burst on the road

to teach the algorithm
that the car should have slowed
right down
to the speed of life,

because you can teach a car to be anything
you want—

these days a car can grow up to be
a model citizen

with a fear of
the vengeance of small things
and a healthy concern
for what is concerning.

This is what we call deep learning.

Abandoned Duckling
in the Car on the Way
to the Animal Hospital

It's hardly worth holding your head up—
that's what someone *else*
might tell you, duckling,
my new favourite weakling.
Not me. Pant away,
but look ahead!
Ahead is the future
and some cumulonimbus clouds.
The world is a set-up,
and I'm someone who melts
for everything vulnerable.
I am emotional caramel,
the colour of your head
resting on my left hand.
Those cumulonimbus clouds understand
rest, reclining on the high ground.
On the second or third attempt
you'll shake off your stupor
with an intuitive nibble
and do what you're able to.
You'll be great at being helped.
You're why
I practise new ways
to say goodbye.

The Dead Men of 2012

For J.M. and T.A.

Like sixpences tumbling to the sea floor

these men live slowly, half on the street,

half behind one window with one plant in it.

They live wherever it's cheaper:

where they've always lived or where there's someone kind.

They live in a city without their children in it.

They live self-antagonisingly, in a kind

of bland fugue, forgiving everyone but themselves.

They drink beer instead of vodka, even though vodka's cheaper.

This counts as 'being nice to themselves'.

They are weeds unfurling their petals by night, soft toys left
    on the floor.

You could greet these men and the sundown

at the same time walking home on 45th Street,

but no, the poem doesn't end with a lovely sundown.

The Invention of the Shovel

They had all seen what digging was like before the shovel.
With trembling fingers, cold from the cold soil, the shovel-less dug,
making scoops of their hands like halved, sucked-out grapefruits,
and about as useful. They were incensed, the pitiable turners
    of earth
who did not have shovels. The compacted dirt under their nails
wouldn't budge. Their fingertips and calluses were one.
They sang of the darkness of the dirt and the darkness of the work.
'Why must we dig inadequately?' they heckled the priests in
    the temples.
'The gods do not will us to drink without bowls or to cook
    without flames
or the fruit-bursting sun. Speak the truth: what is their will?
Is it to use merely the hand, the stick, the bone, the shell?'
And they saw how in the next season there came to them
    the shovel,
with its shaft and its blade like sharp muscles for cleaving roots
and cutting the fields out of their fallowness. They prospered,
and they mastered what they could. And when there came
    among them
some who questioned if this was really the gods' will—
to dominate, to tame, to do the work of priests before the earth's—
they paused. They wondered if the shovel might be a threat.
But they couldn't bring themselves to bury it.

Activism

When you try to explain

what you're doing,

you fall back on metaphors

of animals in distress:

going out in high winds

to catch birds' eggs

blown from nests.

Post-Pandemic Adaptation

I got so distracted by the excitement of
'not going back to the way things were'
that I accidentally went back to the way
things were. I meant to continue working remotely
but instead I book a commercial flight
whenever I go to the office or the supermarket.
I thought I was letting nature heal
but I find myself chasing bees away from flowers
wearing a hornet onesie. I'm only human—
extravagantly, embarrassingly human—
using my breadfruit-weight brain and opposable thumbs
to keep things the same or change them,
whichever one benefits me personally.
Well-meaning people say 'Don't beat yourself up'
but for my villainy I should thrash myself to within an inch
of my spirit leaking from my nose like
a vaporous neon mannequin as I lie on the grass,
inert from my self-battering, the soft sounds
of my breathing rising and falling in time
with the sounds of back-to-normal traffic.

Anxiety and
Executive Function

I'm talking to book-reading friends
who say they can't read
anymore
their minds
are pure
neuronless
gunge

they can't focus
and if they could
they'd focus
on dolphins
or exotic fruit
or flirting

even in the
having-an-attention-span times
no one wrote a book
that could go
toe to toe
with a weirdly attractive
stranger's smile

never mind now
when trying to absorb
meaningful words
is like giving a speech
while having your feet
tickled

I'm sure that books will be
ready for us
whenever we're ready to return to them
like Jesus
or Las Vegas

friends
let's promise
that when that welcome second comes
we look back
and we blame the world
for what went wrong
and not ourselves

Beginning of a Longish Holiday

So: the average cordless drill is used
for thirteen minutes in its lifetime, in case
you think that *your* abilities are squandered.
They are, of course. I'd like to see you grow
prize-winning cauliflowers or be the first
to domesticate the wasp instead of this—
whatever it is we do. At least it's work
and counts as such in the labour statistics,
our simple jobs slumbering unnoticed there
like pet skeletons buried in the garden.
But still, I sometimes think that if we went
together to a choppy, chilly harbour
and swam, just swam, for weeks' worth of weekends,
we'd find our use as manic storytellers,
enhancing first the choppiness and then
the chilliness of the harbour until we
were telling anyone who'd listen that
we had defied nature's many and terrible powers
and were not, in fact, just people in wet towels.
Search the listings for a little coastal village
where the hills are steep and the affect is flat,
where you can still know the good lies from the bad.

Grief Sonnet 1 of 235

There's something nameless at the centre of

a grief, like a hiker seen through binoculars

who could be an electrician called Augustus

or a debt-haunted artist called Zuzanna,

and the more you look at the grief, which for

our purposes is a distant, blurry walker,

the more you transfer your distinct ideas

to the figure processing alone across

the darkening upland to a nearish carpark

or to a village of familiar companions

and adversaries who make up the fully

realised inner world of the namelessness.

All you can bring to this are your roadside guesses.

Is it really so unknowable? That sound you hear is yeses.

Composite Sketch of My Enemy

We are asking all members of the public
to be on the lookout for
a bluff, chuffed eager geezer
who's got the unearned charm of a stolen hotel towel.
Who is as cavalier about taking up your time
as the broad vowels in the phrase 'offshore accounting'.
Who wears two rings on each pinkie
and has eyebrows like the filling of sausage rolls.
Who is between forty and four hundred years old
to judge by his sado-erotic philosophy.
Who may be heard saying things like
'I live in a post-racial world—
the only colour I see is *gold*.'
Who thinks of history as a toy glider—
something to be thrown into a field.
Who would like to see natural law repealed.
Who uses bath bombs in the shower.
Who's had some interesting thoughts
about Foucauldian biopower
as he buys up the supplements aisle.
Who is not a 'lover of wine' but an 'oenophile'.
Who is not a 'lover of folders full of spreadsheets'
but a 'fileophile'.
Who should go seasteading
or on a five-year paintballing weekend
to give his ex-kids and soon-to-be partner a break.
Who is like Christ in the desert,
tempted by Satan to turn stones into bread,
except *he* gives in to the temptation
and sells the heavy loaves as 'Satan cakes'.

He was last seen at 8:30 on Monday morning
heading into a newly opened office block
that looks like a fridge in a moonbeam.
He was seen treating himself to a coffee-flavoured kombucha.
He was seen treating powerful monsters with great respect.
He was seen saying we should treat the poor
with experimental drugs.

If you see this man, do not approach him.
You don't know what sort of dangerous mateyness to expect, so
call in the biohazard team.
Call in the serious strategists drinking tea out of serious mugs.
Call in an airstrike.
Call in a tax hike.
Call in the prick-sniffing dogs.
Call in a therapy chimp to give him a hug.

Information leading to his capture
will be rewarded at the going rate:
a used copy of *The Path to Power* by Margaret Thatcher
and a Fyre Festival commemorative plate.

Cemetery-Going

The face people make when I say I love going to cemeteries
is like the face I make when people say they *don't*
love going to cemeteries: 😐 . It's the only real estate
I aspire to own. I like elderly neighbours. Quiet, reliable, born
in 1891, drowned in the wreck of a ship called *Royal Eucalyptus*,
had family who chose sans-serif lettering. My kind of folks.
Fit all their achievements in a few lines instead of going on and on
about them. If only the rest of the common run could be more
like Silas Albert Whitlow or Henrietta June Baxter, who departed
this life and left behind black slabs and homely couplets
and nostalgia-shaped holes. If you pace these croquet lawns
for the unliving often enough, they start to look like sculpture parks
where every artwork is a life collapsed into a smartly hewn block
like a parochial neutron star. When the gravestones are so polished
you can see your face in them, that's when you know
it's time to think about yourself. And when they're roughened
by lichen and erosion, that's when you know it's time
to think about mysteries: the unknowability of others,
the darkness of motives, the paths unchosen.

Beaches You Can Drown At

On the way there, we have to repeatedly stop
so I can drag lonesome possum corpses
off the road like it's my job.
I don't know what this beach will be like—
I didn't look it up—

looking things up is the enemy
of spontaneous experience-making,
I insist—and it turns out it's another one
of those bits of land improbably cut out
from surrounding steep hills, with ankle-breaking

rocks all the way out to the continental shelf
for all I know. Some maniacs come here to camp.
The current pulls you out with unchivalrous paws.
Even on the shore your lungs feel damp.
We come to these places because

we know others have.
They claimed they could prove it was fun;
they knew what fun was and that fun
was a fungible commodity—it can be multiplied with ease,
you can make ten million funs

if you play the high-stakes game,
if you take your family out
to the wind-blasted, sucking, menacing seaside
and say: *This shivering we feel distinguishes today*
from other days. This is why we came.

Fun is a pyramid scheme,
like all culture. Convince others that the non-reconciling
figures work, wave away the doubts,
build the shonky sandcastle someone saw in a dream,
never be the one who isn't smiling.

Father's Day

When your two sick parents call you
instead of you calling them,
and they tell you they've been taking care
of each other in turn, and you realise:
huh, that's all the parents you've got—
two—you don't have any others
hidden in a bottle at the back of
the cupboard or wrapped in plastic
underneath the bottom drawer,
and no one with mainstream respectability
is going to sell you any parents, either.
No, so maybe two was enough
all along, an amount that made you
deliriously safe for a while,
intangibly bulwarked against menaces
you'll only understand later, if ever.
When the intoxicating effect of protection
wears off and you're vulnerable,
open to stimuli like a drain,
anxiety feels like provocation
and provocation feels like invasion
and the thought of being on your own
makes a confronting, haunting music,
like marbles dropping on a xylophone.

We're Nice to Each Other
After the Trauma

Christchurch, after 15 March 2019

We're nice to each other after the trauma.
It's emotional labour spent in a good cause,
like signing a birthday card at work or volunteering
to clean a beach. In the geography of care
the grieving city is bright, busy, sensitive
to extraordinary needs, able to flex and soothe.
It's one of a series of temporary truths,
a glimpse of something not quite representative
that we wish could stay once it's there.
We wish we couldn't see it disappearing
into routine, because we were desolately happy *because*
we were nice to each other after the trauma.

Shin-Deep in the Floodwaters, Already Afraid

If it was flowing
six inches of this water
could knock me off my feet

floodwater moving
at four miles per hour
would hit me
with the same force
per unit area
as a pillowcase full of doorknobs
dropped from a six-storey building

for now
I'm just in my wellies
gawping at river spillover
out of curiosity
like a traveller here
in this leafy suburb
to see a nightflower
that blooms
once a year

I don't *need* to be here
I can leave whenever I want
I'm about to leave, actually

because I've set boundaries
for myself
like, I'm really not cool with drowning
my safeword is 'oh my God, the water'
but I had to know first-hand

what a little bit of disaster
looks like near home

a tasting-menu amount of emergency
for the finicky and faint-hearted
like me
who live
an uncomforting
couple of feet higher up

it's important to be exposed
to the new culture
so I've got something to talk about
in the long afternoons
in the busy, busy rain

Notes and Acknowledgements

page 7: Ernest Dowson, 'A Last Word', in *Decorations: In Verse and Prose* (Leonard Smithers, 1899), 39.

—Ernst Fischer, *The Necessity of Art: A Marxist Approach* (Penguin, 1963), 72.

—George Monbiot, 'Dare to Declare Capitalism Dead—Before It Takes Us All Down with It', *Guardian*, 25 April 2019. theguardian.com/commentisfree/2019/apr/25/capitalism-economic-system-survival-earth. Lines reproduced with kind permission.

page 39: Wendy Trevino, Sonnet 24 in 'Popular Culture & Cruel Work', *Cruel Fiction* (Commune Editions, 2018), 66. Lines reproduced with kind permission.

—G.A. Cohen, *If You're an Egalitarian, How Come You're So Rich?* Cambridge, Mass.: Harvard University Press, copyright © 2000 by the President and Fellows of Harvard College. Used by permission. All rights reserved.

'Phosphate from Western Sahara' was originally published online in *Milly Magazine* in November of 2020 but was taken down after the editor received numerous threats from anti–Western Sahara liberation trolls. I am proud to have written a poem that pissed off colonialist reactionaries half a world away, and I'm only sorry that its publication had consequences for anyone else.

'Nineteenth-Century Rural Road-Builders' was written in response to a photograph by Henry Thomas Lock: 'View from top of upper incline, looking down towards sea', 1880, albumen print, 190 × 238 mm, Museum of New Zealand Te Papa Tongarewa, O.002179. collections.tepapa.govt.nz/object/201073

The opening of 'The Autonomous Vehicle Research Centre' ('There is only one / really serious philosophical problem / and that is: // do self-driving cars brake for animals?') is a reformulation of the famous (human-centric) proposition by Camus: 'There is only one really serious philosophical problem, and that is suicide.'

The title of 'We're Nice to Each Other After the Trauma' is a slightly distorted echo of Ilya Kaminsky's 'We Lived Happily During the War', in *Deaf Republic* (Graywolf Press, 2019).

Poems in this book have appeared in the following journals:

ANNEXE: 'Composite Sketch of My Enemy'

B O D Y: 'Four Life Forms', 'Nineteenth-Century Rural Road-Builders'

Catalyst: 'The First Plant Grown on the Moon', 'Focus Group Survivor', 'Van Advertising "Interior Plantscaping Services"', 'The Invention of the Shovel'

Cordite: 'Early Evening at the Coal Plant'

descant: 'The Safety Coffin'

FENCE: 'The Please Stop Killing Us and Destroying Everything That Sustains Us Society'

Heavy Feather Review: 'Satellite Insurance'

Landfall: 'All Holidays Are Made-Up Holidays', 'Official Printer to the Government', 'Grief Sonnet 1 of 235'

Love in the Time of COVID: 'Local Politics'

Milly Magazine: 'Phosphate from Western Sahara'

Mimicry: 'Microplastics in Antarctica', 'The Admin Job Psalm'

Minarets: 'The Night Before the Barn-Raising'

The Moth: 'Another Beautiful Day Indoors'

Nine Magazines: 'The Dead Men of 2012'

NZ Poetry Shelf: 'Lives of the Poets', 'We're Nice to Each Other After the Trauma'

petrichor: 'The Autonomous Vehicle Research Centre'

Pine Hills Review: 'Setting up the Debate'

Poetry Ireland Review: 'To a Couple Who Had Their Rings Brought to the Altar by Drone at Their Garden Wedding'

The Quick Brown Dog: 'Picking up Pieces of Paper Other People Have Dropped', 'Activism'

The Spinoff: 'Out on the Pleasure Pier', 'Young Adult Success Stories', 'There Is a Man Dancing on the Rudder of an Enormous Cargo Ship'

Sport: 'The Inertia Poem', 'Agatha and Florian'

Stasis Journal: 'Notes Towards a Definition of Essential Work'

Sweet Mammalian: 'Beginning of a Longish Holiday'

Thanks

Thanks to Meredith Henderson.

Thanks to first readers and critgroup friends: Wade Bishop, Laura Borrowdale, Teresa Correia, Michelle Elvy, Stephanie Hacksley, Rose Journeaux, Melanie McKerchar, John Newton, Amy Paulussen, Chris Stewart, Kat Townley, and Annabel Wilson.

Thanks to Jordan Hamel, Rebecca Hawkes, and essa may ranapiri, who co-edited a book of climate change poems with me and helped me learn new things about poetry and Poetryland throughout the process.

Thanks to the heroes running poetry events in Canterbury and online during some difficult years. A non-exhaustive list includes Andy Coyle, Doc Drumheller, Ciaran Fox, RikTheMost, Ray Shipley, the committee of the Canterbury Poets Collective, Scorpio Books, the Space Academy, and WORD Christchurch. Thanks also to my fellow board members at *takahē*.

Thanks to various people in the orbit of the University of Canterbury over the last few years: Philip Armstrong, Behrouz Boochani, Nathan Joe, Vana Manasiadis, Emanuel Stoakes, Nicholas Wright.

Thanks, THWUP!

Thanks to my friends and comrades in Extinction Rebellion Ōtautahi, who understand what it is like to care until it hurts.

Solidarity with environmental guardians and those in the struggle everywhere.